Pathway to Financial Freedom: Unlocking a Life of Abundance

Table of Contents

1. **Introduction: The Meaning of Financial Freedom**
   - What is financial freedom?
   - Why financial independence matters
   - My journey to financial freedom
2. **Chapter 1: Understanding Money**
   - Money as a tool, not a goal
   - Shifting your mindset about wealth
   - The power of financial literacy
3. **Chapter 2: Setting the Foundation**
   - Establishing your financial goals
   - The importance of budgeting
   - Building an emergency fund
4. **Chapter 3: Overcoming Debt**
   - Types of debt: Good debt vs. bad debt
   - Strategies to eliminate debt (e.g., snowball and avalanche methods)
   - Staying debt-free
5. **Chapter 4: Creating Multiple Income Streams**
   - The power of diversified income
   - Passive income ideas: Investments, royalties, real estate
   - Side hustles: Leveraging your skills and hobbies
6. **Chapter 5: Mastering Investments**
   - Investing basics: Stocks, bonds, and mutual funds
   - Index funds vs. active management
   - Real estate as a path to wealth
   - Understanding risk and reward
7. **Chapter 6: Spending Wisely**
   - Conscious consumption: Needs vs. wants

- Delayed gratification: The key to lasting wealth
- The minimalist approach to finances

8. **Chapter 7: Building Wealth**
    - The magic of compound interest
    - Setting long-term financial goals
    - Retirement planning: Start early, live comfortably

9. **Chapter 8: Protecting Your Assets**
    - The importance of insurance
    - Building a will and estate planning
    - Preparing for unexpected life events

10. **Chapter 9: Cultivating a Wealth Mindset**
    - The psychology of money
    - Overcoming financial anxiety
    - The role of gratitude and generosity in wealth building

11. **Chapter 10: Living a Life of Abundance**
    - Redefining success beyond money
    - The balance between wealth and happiness
    - Sharing your financial wisdom with others

12. **Conclusion: Your Financial Freedom Journey**
    - Reflecting on your progress
    - Staying motivated and consistent
    - Inspiring others on the path to financial freedom

Introduction: The Meaning of Financial Freedom

"Money is a terrible master but an excellent servant." —P.T. Barnum

Financial freedom is more than just having enough money to pay your bills; it's about having the ability to live the life you want without financial stress. It means having the resources to pursue your passions, care for your loved ones, and contribute to causes you believe in.

In this book, you will learn how to take control of your finances, eliminate debt, and build wealth through strategic investments and mindful spending. Whether you're just starting your journey or looking to refine your strategy, this guide offers actionable steps to help you achieve your goals.

Chapter 1: Understanding Money

Money is often viewed with mixed emotions—fear, desire, confusion, and even resentment. Yet, understanding money is the first step on your journey to financial freedom. This chapter will help you redefine your relationship with money, see it as a tool rather than a source of stress, and equip you with the mindset to manage it effectively.

The Purpose of Money

Money, at its core, is a tool—a medium of exchange that enables you to acquire goods and services, achieve goals, and create opportunities. However, society often places an emotional weight on money that complicates our ability to handle it wisely.

Ask yourself:

- How do I feel about money?
- What role has money played in my life so far?
- Have my experiences shaped a positive or negative mindset about wealth?

By reflecting on these questions, you'll uncover the beliefs and emotions that guide your financial decisions.

Shifting Your Mindset About Wealth

Many people grow up with limiting beliefs about money:

- "Money is the root of all evil."
- "Rich people are greedy."
- "I'll never have enough money."

These thoughts create barriers to achieving financial freedom. Instead, adopt empowering beliefs such as:

- "Money is a resource that can be used for good."
- "Wealth allows me to create security and opportunities for myself and others."
- "I am capable of earning, managing, and growing my money."

Remember, wealth is not about how much you earn but how you manage what you have.

Financial Literacy: Your Secret Weapon

Financial literacy is the foundation of money management. It involves understanding basic concepts like budgeting, saving, investing, and debt management. Unfortunately, many people lack these skills, which leaves them vulnerable to financial struggles.

Start by learning the basics:

- **Income:** Know your sources and ensure they exceed your expenses.

- **Expenses:** Track where your money goes to identify areas of improvement.
- **Savings:** Build a habit of setting aside a portion of your income.
- **Debt:** Understand the cost of borrowing and develop strategies to eliminate it.

There are plenty of free resources—books, podcasts, online courses—that can help you build financial literacy step by step.

The Power of Financial Clarity

One of the first actionable steps toward financial freedom is achieving clarity about your current financial situation. Here's how:

1. **Calculate Your Net Worth:**
   Net worth = Total assets - Total liabilities
   Assets include savings, investments, property, and valuables. Liabilities include debts like loans and credit card balances.
2. **Track Your Spending:**
   For one month, record every dollar you spend. Use an app or a simple spreadsheet to categorize your expenses (e.g., groceries, transportation, entertainment).
3. **Identify Your Financial Goals:**
   Write down short-term (saving for a vacation), mid-term (buying a car), and long-term goals (retirement). Be specific and realistic.

Money Myths You Must Let Go Of

As you start to understand money, it's crucial to dispel common myths that hold many people back:

- **Myth:** "I need to earn more to save."
    - **Truth:** Saving starts with managing what you already have.
- **Myth:** "Investing is only for the wealthy."
    - **Truth:** Anyone can invest with small amounts and watch their money grow over time.
- **Myth:** "Debt is unavoidable."
    - **Truth:** While some debts (like a mortgage) may be strategic, most consumer debts can and should be avoided.

The Journey Ahead

Understanding money is a lifelong journey. Start small, be consistent, and celebrate your wins along the way. The more you educate yourself, the more confident you'll feel about managing your finances and achieving financial freedom.

Remember, financial freedom is not about perfection; it's about progress. In the next chapter, we'll lay the groundwork for your financial transformation by setting clear goals and creating a budget that works for you.

Action Steps for Chapter 1:

1. Write down your beliefs about money and identify which ones need to change.
2. Calculate your net worth and track your spending for a month.
3. Choose one financial literacy resource to start learning (a book, podcast, or course).

By the end of this chapter, you'll have a clearer understanding of your financial starting point and the mindset needed to move forward.

Chapter 2: Setting the Foundation

"A goal without a plan is just a wish." —Antoine de Saint-Exupéry

Financial freedom begins with a solid foundation, and the bedrock of that foundation is clear goals and a well-crafted plan. This chapter focuses on helping you define your financial objectives, build a practical budget, and establish an emergency fund to prepare for life's uncertainties.

The Importance of Financial Goals

Before you can achieve financial freedom, you need to know what it looks like for you. Your goals should reflect your personal values, priorities, and dreams.

Three Types of Financial Goals:

1. **Short-Term Goals (0–2 years):**
    - Examples: Paying off credit card debt, saving for a vacation, or creating an emergency fund.
2. **Mid-Term Goals (2–10 years):**
    - Examples: Buying a car, saving for a home down payment, or starting a business.
3. **Long-Term Goals (10+ years):**
    - Examples: Building retirement savings, paying off your mortgage, or creating a legacy fund for your children.

Setting SMART Goals

Make your goals **SMART**: Specific, Measurable, Achievable, Relevant, and Time-bound.

- **Specific:** "Save $5,000 for a family vacation" is better than "Save for vacation."
- **Measurable:** Track progress—"Save $500 per month for 10 months."
- **Achievable:** Be realistic based on your income and expenses.
- **Relevant:** Ensure the goal aligns with your values and priorities.
- **Time-bound:** Set a deadline to create urgency and focus.

Creating a Budget That Works

A budget is your financial blueprint. It helps you allocate your income toward essential expenses, savings, and goals.

Steps to Create a Budget:

1. **Track Your Income:** Know how much you earn each month after taxes. Include all sources of income, like salary, freelance work, or investments.
2. **List Your Expenses:** Break them into categories:
    - Fixed (rent, utilities, insurance)

- Variable (groceries, entertainment, dining out)
- Periodic (gifts, annual subscriptions)
3. **Set Spending Limits:** Assign a maximum amount for each category based on your income.
4. **Prioritize Savings:** Save first, spend later. A good rule of thumb is the **50/30/20 rule**:
    - 50% for needs (housing, food, transportation)
    - 30% for wants (entertainment, travel)
    - 20% for savings and debt repayment
5. **Review Regularly:** Life changes—so should your budget. Review it monthly to ensure it still fits your financial situation and goals.

Building an Emergency Fund

An emergency fund is a safety net for unexpected expenses, like medical bills, car repairs, or job loss. Without one, financial setbacks can lead to debt or derail your progress.

How Much Should You Save?

- Start with a goal of **$1,000** for immediate emergencies.
- Aim to save **3–6 months of living expenses** over time.

Where to Keep Your Emergency Fund:

- Use a high-yield savings account for easy access and growth.

- Avoid tying it up in investments or accounts with withdrawal penalties.

Common Budgeting Pitfalls and How to Avoid Them

1. **Being Too Strict:**
    - Allow some flexibility. Leave room for fun and unexpected expenses.
2. **Ignoring Small Expenses:**
    - Little costs add up. Review your subscriptions, daily coffee, or impulse purchases.
3. **Not Tracking Spending:**
    - Use apps or spreadsheets to monitor your spending habits.
4. **Skipping Regular Updates:**
    - Adjust your budget when your income or expenses change.

A Plan for Every Dollar

Every dollar you earn should have a purpose—whether it's for savings, paying bills, or investing. This concept, known as zero-based budgeting, ensures you're intentional with your money. At the end of the month, your income minus expenses should equal zero because every dollar is allocated somewhere.

The Power of Consistency

Budgeting and saving may seem tedious at first, but consistency is key. Over time, these habits become second nature, and the rewards compound. You'll find yourself better prepared for challenges and closer to achieving your goals.

Your Financial Foundation Checklist

By the end of this chapter, you should:

1. Have clearly defined **short-, mid-, and long-term financial goals**.
2. Create and stick to a **realistic budget**.
3. Start or build an **emergency fund**.

These steps lay the groundwork for financial success, empowering you to take control of your money and focus on growing your wealth in the next chapter.

In the upcoming chapter, we'll dive into strategies for tackling debt and freeing yourself from financial burdens that hinder your progress. The journey to financial freedom continues!

Chapter 3: Escaping the Debt Trap

"You can't out-earn bad spending habits." —Dave Ramsey

Debt is one of the most significant obstacles to financial freedom. While some debt can be strategic (like a mortgage or student loan), most forms of consumer debt are burdens that weigh heavily on your finances and future. This chapter will teach you how to escape the debt trap, avoid falling back into it, and build a debt-free lifestyle.

Understanding Debt: Good vs. Bad

Not all debt is created equal. Some types of debt can serve a purpose, while others create unnecessary financial strain.

Good Debt:

- Used to finance assets that grow in value or generate income.
    - Examples:
        - Mortgage loans (building equity in a home).
        - Student loans (investing in education for better job prospects).

Bad Debt:

- Used to purchase liabilities or items that depreciate in value.
    - Examples:
        - Credit card debt from non-essential spending.
        - Payday loans with exorbitant interest rates.

The True Cost of Debt

Debt isn't just the amount you borrow—it's the interest and fees that accumulate over time. Many people underestimate how much debt costs them.

Example of Interest Costs:

- Credit card balance: $5,000
- Interest rate: 20%
- Minimum payment: $100/month

At this rate, it would take over 6 years to pay off the debt, costing you nearly $4,500 in interest!

Understanding this hidden cost can motivate you to tackle debt aggressively.

Step 1: Assess Your Debt Situation

Start by getting a clear picture of what you owe.

Create a Debt Inventory:

1. List all debts: credit cards, personal loans, student loans, car loans, etc.
2. Include the following for each:
    - Balance owed.
    - Interest rate.
    - Minimum payment.
    - Due date.

This overview helps you prioritize and plan your repayment strategy.

Step 2: Choose a Debt Repayment Strategy

There are two popular methods for paying off debt:

1. Debt Snowball Method:

- Focus on paying off the smallest debt first while making minimum payments on others.
- Once the smallest debt is cleared, apply that payment amount to the next smallest debt.
- Benefit: Quick wins keep you motivated.

2. Debt Avalanche Method:

- Focus on paying off the debt with the highest interest rate first while making minimum payments on others.
- Once the highest-interest debt is cleared, move to the next highest.
- Benefit: Saves money on interest in the long run.

Both methods work—choose the one that feels right for you.

Step 3: Reduce Expenses to Free Up Cash

To accelerate debt repayment, you'll need to create extra room in your budget.

Ways to Cut Costs:

- Cancel unused subscriptions.
- Cook at home instead of dining out.
- Limit impulse purchases by using a shopping list.
- Shop for discounts or use cashback apps.

Boost Your Income:

- Take on a part-time job or freelance gig.
- Sell unused items online.
- Use cashback rewards or loyalty programs wisely.

Step 4: Negotiate and Refinance

Debt doesn't have to be static. Explore ways to lower your interest rates or consolidate loans.

Options to Consider:

1. **Negotiate with Creditors:**
   - Call and request a lower interest rate or payment plan.
   - Some companies offer hardship programs.
2. **Debt Consolidation Loans:**
   - Combine multiple debts into a single loan with a lower interest rate.
3. **Balance Transfer Credit Cards:**
   - Transfer high-interest balances to a card with a 0% introductory rate.
   - Be cautious of transfer fees and promotional period deadlines.

Step 5: Build New Habits to Avoid Future Debt

Getting out of debt is only half the battle. Staying out of debt requires changing the habits and mindsets that led to it.

Practical Tips:

- **Save Before You Spend:** Build an emergency fund to cover unexpected expenses.
- **Use Cash or Debit:** Avoid credit unless you can pay the balance in full each month.
- **Plan Big Purchases:** Save up for items instead of financing them.
- **Avoid Lifestyle Inflation:** As your income grows, keep your spending in check.

Step 6: Celebrate Milestones

Paying off debt is a significant achievement—don't forget to celebrate your progress.

- Treat yourself modestly when you pay off each debt.
- Share your victories with supportive friends or family.

Celebrating milestones keeps you motivated and focused on the end goal: financial freedom.

Breaking the Debt Cycle

Debt can feel like a trap, but you hold the key to break free. By taking deliberate steps, staying disciplined, and focusing on your goals, you can regain control of your finances and start building a debt-free future.

Action Steps for Chapter 3:

1. Create a debt inventory and choose a repayment strategy (snowball or avalanche).
2. Cut unnecessary expenses and look for ways to increase your income.
3. Explore options to lower your interest rates or consolidate debts.
4. Commit to building habits that prevent future debt.

In the next chapter, we'll explore the power of saving and investing, and how to make your money work for you. With your debt under control, you're ready to grow your wealth and secure your financial future. The best is yet to come!

Chapter 4: Building Wealth Through Saving and Investing

"Don't work for money; make money work for you." —Robert Kiyosaki

Now that you've tackled your debt, it's time to shift your focus from survival to growth. Saving and investing are the keys to building wealth and achieving financial freedom. In this chapter, we'll explore how to save effectively, understand the basics of investing, and use these tools to grow your wealth over time.

The Power of Saving

Saving money is the cornerstone of financial security. It provides a cushion for unexpected expenses, funds your goals, and creates the capital needed for investments.

Why Saving Matters

1. **Emergency Preparedness:** Protect yourself from life's surprises, like medical bills or car repairs.
2. **Goal Achievement:** Fund dreams like vacations, buying a home, or starting a business.
3. **Investment Capital:** Savings fuel investments, which in turn generate passive income.

Steps to Save More Effectively

1. Pay Yourself First

Treat savings like a non-negotiable expense. Allocate a percentage of your income to savings before paying for anything else. Start with 10%–20% and adjust as needed.

2. Automate Your Savings

Set up automatic transfers to a dedicated savings account. This removes the temptation to spend before saving.

3. Cut Costs on Non-Essentials

Review your budget for areas to reduce spending. For example:

- Cancel unused subscriptions.
- Cook at home instead of eating out.
- Opt for generic brands instead of name brands.

4. Take Advantage of Windfalls

Whenever you receive unexpected money (bonuses, tax refunds, gifts), save or invest a significant portion.

Understanding Investing

Investing is the process of putting your money into assets that have the potential to grow over time. While saving is essential for stability, investing is what accelerates wealth-building.

Why Invest?

- **Beat Inflation:** Inflation erodes the purchasing power of money. Investing helps your money grow faster than inflation.
- **Build Wealth:** Investments compound over time, creating exponential growth.
- **Create Passive Income:** Certain investments, like stocks or real estate, generate income without active effort.

The Basics of Investing

1. Start with the Right Mindset

- **Long-Term Thinking:** Investing is a marathon, not a sprint. Patience is key.
- **Accept Risk:** All investments carry some level of risk. Understand your risk tolerance before diving in.

2. Understand the Asset Classes

- **Stocks:** Ownership in a company; potential for high returns but higher risk.
- **Bonds:** Loans to companies or governments; lower returns but more stable.
- **Real Estate:** Tangible assets that generate rental income or appreciate in value.
- **Mutual Funds/ETFs:** Diversified investments managed by professionals.

- **Cash and Equivalents:** Savings accounts or money market funds; low risk, low return.

3. Diversify Your Investments

Don't put all your eggs in one basket. Spread your money across various asset classes to reduce risk.

4. Leverage Tax-Advantaged Accounts

- Use retirement accounts like IRAs, 401(k)s, or their international equivalents to grow wealth tax-free or tax-deferred.
- Research government programs or incentives available in your country.

The Power of Compound Interest

Albert Einstein once called compound interest "the eighth wonder of the world." Here's why:

How It Works:

- When you earn returns on both your principal and previously earned returns, your money grows exponentially over time.

Example:

- Investing $200/month at an average return of 8% for 30 years grows to nearly $300,000.

The earlier you start investing, the more time compounding works in your favor.

How to Get Started with Investing

1. **Educate Yourself:**
   - Read books, take courses, and follow trusted financial experts.
   - Understand basic terms like ROI (Return on Investment), diversification, and risk tolerance.
2. **Start Small:**
   - Begin with an amount you're comfortable with, even if it's just $50/month.
3. **Use Investment Platforms:**
   - Online brokers or robo-advisors make investing accessible for beginners.
4. **Seek Professional Advice:**
   - If you're unsure where to start, consult a financial advisor to help create a personalized investment plan.

Balancing Saving and Investing

It's important to strike the right balance between saving and investing. Here's a guideline:

1. Build an emergency fund (3–6 months of living expenses) first.
2. Save for short-term goals in low-risk accounts.
3. Invest for long-term goals like retirement or wealth accumulation.

Avoid Common Pitfalls

1. **Investing Without Research:**
   - Never put money into something you don't understand.
2. **Chasing High Returns:**
   - Investments promising unrealistically high returns are often scams.
3. **Timing the Market:**
   - Focus on time *in* the market, not timing it. Consistent investing yields better results.
4. **Neglecting Fees:**
   - High fees can eat into your returns. Compare platforms and investment options for cost-effectiveness.

The Road Ahead

Saving and investing require discipline and patience, but the rewards are life-changing. As your wealth grows, so does your freedom—freedom to make choices without financial constraints, freedom to support your family and dreams, and freedom to give back to your community.

Action Steps for Chapter 4:

1. Set a monthly savings goal and automate it.
2. Begin learning about investment options that align with your risk tolerance and goals.

3. Start investing, even with a small amount, and commit to consistency.

In the next chapter, we'll dive into the art of passive income and how to create multiple streams of revenue, allowing your wealth to grow even when you're not actively working. The journey to financial independence is just getting started!

Chapter 5: Unlocking Passive Income

"If you don't find a way to make money while you sleep, you will work until you die." —Warren Buffett

Passive income is the holy grail of financial freedom. It allows you to generate money without constant effort, giving you the freedom to focus on what matters most in life. This chapter explores the different types of passive income, how to build multiple streams, and why it's a game-changer in your wealth-building journey.

What Is Passive Income?

Passive income is money earned with minimal effort after the initial work or investment is complete. Unlike active income, where you trade time for money, passive income works for you even when you're not actively involved.

Examples of Passive Income:

1. Rental income from properties.
2. Dividends from stocks.
3. Royalties from books, music, or online courses.
4. Revenue from a business you don't actively manage.

Why Passive Income Is Essential

1. **Financial Independence:** Passive income reduces reliance on a single paycheck, providing financial security.
2. **Time Freedom:** It frees you from trading time for money, allowing you to pursue passions, hobbies, or family time.
3. **Wealth Accumulation:** With consistent reinvestment, passive income streams grow exponentially over time.

Step 1: Identify Your Strengths and Resources

Building passive income starts with understanding your unique resources, skills, and interests.

Questions to Consider:

- Do you have savings to invest in income-generating assets?
- Are there skills you can monetize (e.g., writing, teaching, designing)?
- Can you dedicate time upfront to create a product, like an online course or book?
- Are you comfortable with risk, or do you prefer low-risk options?

Your answers will help determine which passive income strategies suit you best.

Step 2: Choose Passive Income Streams

Here are some of the most popular and effective ways to generate passive income:

1. Real Estate

- Buy properties to rent out for consistent cash flow.
- Consider vacation rentals or Airbnb for higher returns.
- Explore Real Estate Investment Trusts (REITs) if you prefer a hands-off approach.

2. Dividend Stocks

- Invest in companies that pay regular dividends.
- Reinvest dividends for compounding growth.
- Look for blue-chip stocks with a history of reliable payouts.

3. Digital Products

- Write an eBook, create an online course, or sell templates.
- Platforms like Amazon Kindle, Udemy, or Etsy make it easy to market and sell your products globally.

4. Peer-to-Peer Lending

- Lend money through platforms that connect borrowers with lenders.
- Earn interest on loans, but be mindful of default risks.

5. Automated Businesses

- Invest in businesses you don't actively manage, such as vending machines, car washes, or drop-shipping e-commerce stores.

6. Intellectual Property

- Earn royalties from patents, trademarks, or creative works (music, photography, or art).

7. Content Creation

- Start a blog, YouTube channel, or podcast.
- Monetize through ads, sponsorships, and affiliate marketing.
- While time-intensive initially, successful content creation can generate income long-term.

Step 3: Build and Scale Your Income Streams

Once you've chosen a passive income strategy, follow these steps to build and grow it:

1. Start Small and Focused

- Avoid spreading yourself too thin. Start with one or two streams and perfect them before diversifying.

2. Reinvest Earnings

- Use initial profits to grow your passive income. For example, reinvest rental income into new properties or dividends into additional stock purchases.

3. Optimize Systems

- Automate processes to reduce the time you spend managing your streams.
- Example: Use property management companies for rentals or hire freelancers to handle digital product updates.

4. Track and Evaluate

- Regularly review your income streams to ensure profitability.
- Drop or improve underperforming ventures.

Step 4: Avoiding Common Pitfalls

Pitfall 1: Expecting Immediate Results

- Passive income often requires significant time and effort upfront. Be patient.

Pitfall 2: Neglecting Due Diligence

- Research thoroughly before investing in any opportunity. Beware of scams promising unrealistic returns.

Pitfall 3: Overextending Finances

- Don't take on excessive debt to fund passive income projects. Start within your means.

Pitfall 4: Ignoring Taxes

- Passive income is taxable. Consult a tax advisor to plan accordingly and take advantage of deductions.

Real-Life Example: The Snowball Effect

Imagine starting with $5,000 in savings. You use this to buy dividend-paying stocks with a 4% annual return. Over the years, you reinvest the dividends, allowing compound growth to take effect. As your portfolio grows, so does your passive income, eventually reaching a point where it covers significant living expenses.

By starting early and staying consistent, even small investments can lead to substantial results.

The Lifestyle Shift

As your passive income grows, you'll notice a shift in your financial and personal life. You may be able to:

- Work fewer hours or retire early.
- Spend more time with loved ones or pursue hobbies.
- Travel or live in locations you've always dreamed of.

The goal is not to escape work entirely but to create options and opportunities that align with your values and goals.

Action Steps for Chapter 5:

1. List your skills, resources, and interests to identify potential passive income streams.
2. Choose one stream and dedicate time to building it over the next 6 months.
3. Reinvest earnings to grow your income.
4. Regularly review and optimize your strategies to maximize results.

In the next chapter, we'll explore how to protect your growing wealth through effective financial planning, insurance, and smart tax strategies. You've worked hard to build your income—now it's time to ensure it lasts for generations.

Chapter 6: Protecting and Preserving Wealth

"It's not how much money you make, but how much money you keep, how hard it works for you, and how many generations you keep it for." —Robert Kiyosaki

Building wealth is only half the journey. The other half involves protecting and preserving what you've earned to secure your financial future and the well-being of your loved ones. In this chapter, we'll cover strategies to safeguard your wealth through smart financial planning, insurance, asset diversification, and estate planning.

The Importance of Wealth Protection

Life is unpredictable, and unforeseen circumstances—whether personal, economic, or natural—can threaten your financial stability. Protecting your wealth ensures that your financial foundation remains intact, even during challenging times.

Key Reasons to Prioritize Wealth Protection:

1. **To Manage Risks:** Shield against unexpected events like job loss, accidents, or economic downturns.
2. **To Preserve Assets:** Avoid erosion of wealth due to poor decisions, lawsuits, or emergencies.

3. **To Ensure Legacy:** Pass on your wealth to future generations without unnecessary legal or tax burdens.

Step 1: Build a Financial Safety Net

Emergency Fund

An emergency fund is your first line of defense against financial shocks. Aim to save 3–6 months' worth of living expenses in a highly liquid and accessible account.

Debt Management

High-interest debt is a major threat to wealth. Prioritize paying off such debts before focusing on aggressive investments.

Step 2: Insure Your Wealth

Insurance is a crucial tool in wealth protection. It acts as a safety net against significant financial losses.

Types of Insurance to Consider:

1. **Health Insurance:** Covers medical expenses and prevents out-of-pocket financial strain during illness or injury.
2. **Life Insurance:** Provides financial security for your dependents in the event of your death.

3. **Disability Insurance:** Protects your income if you're unable to work due to injury or illness.
4. **Property Insurance:** Covers your home, car, or other valuable assets against damage or theft.
5. **Liability Insurance:** Shields you from lawsuits and legal claims that could impact your finances.

Choosing the Right Coverage:

- Evaluate your personal and financial situation.
- Seek advice from a trusted insurance agent or financial planner.
- Regularly review and update policies as your life circumstances change.

Step 3: Diversify Your Assets

Why Diversification Matters:

Diversification spreads risk across different asset classes, reducing the likelihood of catastrophic losses.

How to Diversify:

1. **Across Asset Classes:** Invest in a mix of stocks, bonds, real estate, and alternative assets.
2. **Geographically:** Spread investments across different regions to reduce risk from localized economic downturns.
3. **Industries and Sectors:** Avoid overexposure to a single industry by investing in a broad range of sectors.

Step 4: Protect Against Inflation and Market Volatility

Combatting Inflation:

- Invest in inflation-protected securities (e.g., TIPS).
- Consider real estate or commodities, which tend to appreciate during inflationary periods.

Hedging Market Volatility:

- Maintain a balanced portfolio with a mix of high-risk and low-risk investments.
- Use tools like stop-loss orders or invest in hedging instruments like options if appropriate.

Step 5: Plan for Taxes

Taxes can significantly impact your wealth if not managed effectively.

Tax-Reduction Strategies:

1. **Maximize Tax-Advantaged Accounts:** Contribute to retirement accounts (e.g., 401(k), IRA) or health savings accounts (HSA).
2. **Utilize Tax Credits and Deductions:** Take advantage of eligible credits and write-offs, such as education credits or mortgage interest deductions.

3. **Harvest Tax Losses:** Offset capital gains by selling underperforming assets at a loss.
4. **Consult a Tax Professional:** Stay informed about tax laws and how they impact your financial decisions.

Step 6: Estate Planning for Generational Wealth

Why Estate Planning Is Essential:

Without a proper estate plan, your wealth could be subject to legal disputes or significant taxes, reducing what you pass on to your heirs.

Key Components of an Estate Plan:

1. **Will:** Specifies how your assets will be distributed after your death.
2. **Trusts:** Protect assets from probate and can reduce estate taxes.
3. **Power of Attorney:** Designates someone to make financial or medical decisions if you're unable.
4. **Beneficiary Designations:** Ensure retirement accounts, life insurance, and other assets go to the intended recipients.

Steps to Get Started:

- Work with an estate planning attorney.
- Update your plan regularly to reflect changes in family or financial circumstances.

Step 7: Build a Legacy Through Philanthropy

Giving back can be a meaningful way to protect and grow your wealth while leaving a lasting impact.

Philanthropic Strategies:

1. **Charitable Trusts:** Reduce taxes and create a legacy by supporting causes you care about.
2. **Donor-Advised Funds:** Offer flexibility in donating while enjoying tax benefits.
3. **Family Foundations:** Teach your heirs the value of stewardship through organized giving.

Common Mistakes to Avoid in Wealth Protection

1. **Underinsuring Assets:** Insufficient coverage can lead to devastating financial losses.
2. **Overconcentration:** Putting all your wealth in one asset class, like real estate or stocks, increases risk.
3. **Ignoring Inflation:** Failing to account for inflation can erode your purchasing power over time.
4. **Procrastinating on Estate Planning:** Delaying estate planning can leave your assets vulnerable to disputes or excessive taxes.

Action Steps for Chapter 6:

1. Start or update your emergency fund to cover at least 3 months of expenses.
2. Review your insurance coverage and fill any gaps.
3. Diversify your portfolio across asset classes, regions, and industries.
4. Consult a tax advisor to optimize your tax strategy.
5. Begin or update your estate plan to secure your wealth for future generations.

Looking Ahead:

Protecting and preserving your wealth creates a strong foundation for financial freedom. In the next chapter, we'll dive into *how to teach financial literacy to your family*, ensuring your loved ones continue to build on the legacy you've worked hard to create. Together, we'll ensure that financial freedom becomes a generational reality.

Chapter 7: Teaching Financial Literacy to Your Family

"An investment in knowledge pays the best interest." —Benjamin Franklin

Financial freedom isn't just about achieving your own stability; it's also about empowering the next generation to sustain and grow that wealth. Teaching financial literacy to your family ensures that your legacy of smart money management continues long after you're gone. In this chapter, we'll explore strategies for instilling financial knowledge and responsibility in your family, regardless of age.

Why Financial Literacy Matters for Families

Financially literate families are better equipped to make informed decisions, avoid common pitfalls, and work together toward shared goals. By teaching your loved ones about money, you're fostering a culture of empowerment, accountability, and confidence.

Benefits of Financial Literacy in Families:

- Reduced family conflicts over money.
- Greater financial independence for children and dependents.
- Long-term security for multigenerational wealth.

Step 1: Start with the Basics for Young Children

It's never too early to introduce children to the concept of money.

Simple Lessons for Young Kids:

1. **Understanding Money:** Teach them that money is earned and used to buy things.
2. **Saving and Spending:** Use clear jars or piggy banks to separate "saving," "spending," and "sharing" funds.
3. **Earning Money:** Give them small chores to complete in exchange for an allowance.

Activities to Build Awareness:

- Play pretend shopping games.
- Read children's books about money (e.g., *Bunny Money* by Rosemary Wells).
- Encourage saving for a small toy or treat to teach delayed gratification.

Step 2: Equip Teenagers with Real-World Skills

Teenagers are at a critical stage for learning about money, as they're beginning to navigate independence.

Financial Skills for Teens:

1. **Budgeting:** Show them how to allocate money for needs, wants, and savings.
2. **Banking:** Open a savings account and teach them how to manage deposits and withdrawals.
3. **Earning Income:** Encourage part-time jobs or entrepreneurial ventures.
4. **Understanding Credit:** Explain the basics of credit scores, loans, and debt.

Practical Exercises:

- Have them plan a family outing within a set budget.
- Introduce budgeting apps to track their spending.
- Match their savings contributions to motivate them.

Step 3: Empower Young Adults to Build Independence

For young adults entering college or the workforce, financial literacy becomes even more vital.

Key Lessons for Young Adults:

1. **Living Within Means:** Stress the importance of avoiding lifestyle inflation.
2. **Saving for Emergencies:** Emphasize starting an emergency fund early.
3. **Investing Basics:** Introduce the power of compound interest and long-term investing.
4. **Taxes:** Teach them how to file taxes and understand withholdings.

Strategies to Support Growth:

- Offer guidance without micromanaging.
- Share your own financial successes and mistakes to provide perspective.
- Encourage them to create financial goals, like saving for a car or down payment.

Step 4: Foster a Collaborative Family Approach to Money

Open communication about finances can help your family work together toward shared goals.

Ways to Collaborate:

1. **Family Budgeting Meetings:** Discuss expenses, savings, and financial goals as a family.
2. **Set Joint Goals:** Plan for family vacations, a new home, or other shared aspirations.
3. **Transparency:** Share age-appropriate details about household finances to promote understanding.

Encouraging Good Habits:

- Celebrate milestones like paying off debt or reaching a savings goal.
- Reward behaviors like consistent saving or budgeting.

Step 5: Teach Financial Responsibility Through Generational Wealth

If you've built significant assets, ensure your heirs understand their responsibilities.

Key Lessons for Heirs:

1. **Managing Inheritances:** Teach them how to preserve and grow wealth rather than spend it recklessly.
2. **Philanthropy:** Encourage giving back to the community as part of their financial journey.
3. **Long-Term Thinking:** Emphasize the importance of planning for future generations.

Family Wealth Education:

- Create a family mission statement about financial values and goals.
- Host workshops or invite financial advisors to educate the family.

Step 6: Be a Role Model

Your actions set the tone for your family's relationship with money. Be a living example of financial responsibility.

How to Model Good Habits:

- Stick to a budget and track your expenses.
- Show the importance of saving and giving back.

- Be honest about financial challenges and how you overcome them.

Common Mistakes in Teaching Financial Literacy

1. **Avoiding Money Discussions:** Silence creates uncertainty and misunderstanding.
2. **Bailing Out Poor Decisions:** Rescue missions prevent your family from learning from mistakes.
3. **Imposing Your Choices:** Guide your family without dictating their financial decisions.

Action Steps for Chapter 7:

1. Introduce age-appropriate money lessons to children and teenagers.
2. Open a savings account for each family member and encourage regular contributions.
3. Set up a monthly family meeting to discuss financial goals and progress.
4. Create a family mission statement outlining your financial values.
5. Work with a financial advisor to prepare heirs for managing generational wealth.

Looking Ahead:

Teaching financial literacy isn't just a lesson—it's a gift that keeps giving. As your family becomes more financially confident, they'll take the principles you've instilled and apply them to every stage of life. In the next chapter, we'll explore how to turn *setbacks into opportunities*, equipping you with strategies to bounce back stronger when life throws financial challenges your way.

Chapter 8: Turning Setbacks into Opportunities

"Success is not final, failure is not fatal: It is the courage to continue that counts." —Winston Churchill

In the pursuit of financial freedom, setbacks are inevitable. Whether it's a job loss, a market downturn, or an unexpected financial emergency, life has a way of throwing challenges our way. But the difference between those who achieve financial freedom and those who don't is how they respond to these challenges. In this chapter, we'll explore how to turn setbacks into stepping stones on your path to financial independence.

Understanding Setbacks: The Reality of Life's Financial Curveballs

Setbacks don't mean failure—they're simply part of the journey. When they occur, it's essential to embrace a mindset that views setbacks as opportunities for growth and learning. Every challenge is a chance to strengthen your resilience and refine your approach to managing money.

Common Financial Setbacks:

- **Job Loss or Reduced Income:** A sudden loss of income can feel devastating, but it's also an opportunity to reassess your financial priorities.

- **Unexpected Expenses:** Medical bills, car repairs, or home maintenance can disrupt your budget but can be managed with preparation.
- **Market Volatility:** For those investing in stocks or real estate, market downturns are unavoidable. However, they can be weathered with long-term strategies.
- **Debt:** Whether it's from credit cards, student loans, or other sources, debt is a common financial hurdle. It can be overwhelming, but it's solvable with the right plan.

The Key to Overcoming Setbacks:

Your mindset determines how you move forward. A growth mindset is crucial when dealing with financial challenges. It allows you to see each setback not as a roadblock but as an opportunity to pivot, learn, and adapt.

Step 1: Assess the Situation Calmly and Honestly

When facing a setback, the first step is to stop and evaluate the situation. Panicking or ignoring the problem won't help. Instead, take the time to assess:

- **What happened?** Determine the exact cause of the setback. Was it a result of external circumstances, or could it have been prevented with better planning?
- **How does this affect my financial goals?** Consider the short- and long-term impact on your savings, investments, and lifestyle.

- **What's my immediate response?** Outline the first steps to take in order to stabilize your financial situation, such as cutting unnecessary expenses or seeking temporary income.

Reflection:

Consider how this setback compares to others in your life. Have you faced financial challenges before and come out stronger? Often, setbacks are opportunities to realize how far you've come and what you've learned in the process.

Step 2: Reevaluate Your Financial Plan

Once you've assessed the situation, it's time to rework your financial strategy. This doesn't mean you have to throw out everything you've been doing; instead, look for ways to adapt to the current circumstances.

Re-evaluation Tips:

- **Revisit Your Budget:** Review your budget to see if there are areas where you can cut back or adjust. For example, if you've lost income, temporarily reducing discretionary spending might help.
- **Emergency Fund Use:** If you have an emergency fund, this is exactly what it's for. Use it wisely, but don't deplete it unless necessary.
- **Diversify Your Income Streams:** If your primary source of income is at risk, consider

side jobs, freelance work, or other income-generating activities.
- **Rebalance Investments:** If your investments have taken a hit, it might be time to reassess your risk tolerance. Speak with a financial advisor to ensure that your portfolio matches your current financial goals.

Step 3: Build or Strengthen Your Emergency Fund

An emergency fund is your safety net when things go wrong. If you don't have one already, now is the time to prioritize building it. If you already have one, this may be the time to grow it further.

How to Build an Emergency Fund:

1. **Set a Goal:** Aim for at least three to six months of living expenses in your emergency fund. For those with dependents or unstable incomes, a larger emergency fund may be advisable.
2. **Automate Savings:** Set up automatic transfers to your emergency fund so that you don't have to think about it. Even small, consistent contributions add up over time.
3. **Re-evaluate Your Spending:** Look for areas where you can cut back temporarily in order to build your emergency savings faster.

The Power of an Emergency Fund:

Having this buffer can ease the pressure during financial setbacks, giving you the space to make calm, informed decisions without scrambling for immediate solutions.

Step 4: Use Setbacks as Learning Opportunities

Every setback offers valuable lessons. Instead of dwelling on the negative aspects, focus on what you can learn and how you can improve your financial habits.

Questions to Ask Yourself After a Setback:

- **What could I have done differently to avoid this?**
- **What habits or behaviors led to this situation?**
- **What new knowledge or skills can I acquire to better handle setbacks in the future?**

Turning Lessons into Action:

For example, if you're dealing with high levels of debt, use this experience to learn about debt management strategies, such as the debt snowball or debt avalanche method. If market volatility has affected your investments, take this time to learn about diversification and safer investment options.

Step 5: Stay Focused on Your Long-Term Goals

It's easy to get discouraged in the face of setbacks, but it's important to keep your long-term financial goals in view. Setbacks are temporary, but your financial freedom is a long-term pursuit.

Focus on These Key Strategies:

- **Consistency Over Perfection:** Small, consistent actions often lead to greater long-term results than trying to make large, perfect decisions all at once.
- **Set New Milestones:** Even if your original goals need adjustment, continue to set new, realistic milestones. Celebrate each step you take toward financial recovery and growth.
- **Stay Positive and Persistent:** Adopting a positive attitude toward setbacks makes it easier to stay motivated. Remember, your financial freedom is still possible—just keep moving forward.

Step 6: Leverage Professional Help When Needed

If the setback is significant or you feel overwhelmed, there's no shame in seeking professional advice. Financial advisors, credit counselors, and other experts can help you navigate challenges and come up with strategies tailored to your unique situation.

Types of Professional Help to Consider:

- **Financial Advisors:** For investment or retirement planning advice.
- **Credit Counselors:** If debt management or credit issues are causing setbacks.
- **Accountants or Tax Professionals:** To help you navigate tax implications during financial changes.

Action Steps for Chapter 8:

1. **Take Immediate Action:** If you're facing a setback, calmly assess the situation and take initial steps to stabilize your finances.
2. **Review Your Budget:** Revisit your budget and adjust it to fit your new reality.
3. **Build or Strengthen Your Emergency Fund:** If you don't have one, start building it today.
4. **Learn from the Setback:** Reflect on what you can learn from the experience and use it to adjust your financial approach.
5. **Stay Focused on the Big Picture:** Keep your eyes on your long-term financial goals, remembering that setbacks are just temporary challenges.

Looking Ahead:

Setbacks may feel like obstacles, but they can be some of the most powerful moments for growth on your journey to financial freedom. By assessing, adapting, learning, and staying focused on your long-term goals, you'll find that these challenges ultimately become stepping stones. In the next chapter, we'll look at how to *maximize your income* by exploring various ways to increase your earning potential.

Chapter 9: Maximizing Your Income

"Don't wait for opportunity to knock—create it." — Anonymous

When striving for financial freedom, one of the most effective ways to accelerate your progress is by maximizing your income. While reducing expenses is important, increasing your earning potential creates a much greater impact on your ability to save, invest, and build wealth. In this chapter, we'll explore practical strategies to boost your income, whether through advancing your career, exploring side hustles, or investing in your skills.

Understanding the Importance of Maximizing Income

Many people focus solely on budgeting and cutting back on expenses to achieve financial freedom. However, no matter how much you cut, there will always be a limit to how much you can save. Maximizing your income opens up more opportunities for investing, saving, and achieving your financial goals faster. It's the key to accelerating your journey toward financial independence.

Why Maximizing Income Is Crucial:

- **Increased Savings Potential:** The more you earn, the more you can save and invest for the future.
- **Faster Debt Repayment:** Higher income helps you pay off debt faster, reducing the interest you pay over time.
- **Building Wealth:** Higher earnings mean more capital to invest in assets like stocks, real estate, or businesses.
- **Financial Flexibility:** A higher income provides more freedom in your personal life, allowing you to make choices based on your goals, not your paycheck.

Step 1: Advancing Your Career

One of the most powerful ways to increase your income is by advancing your career. Whether you're currently employed or looking for a new position, focusing on career growth can have a significant impact on your earning potential.

Strategies to Advance Your Career:

1. **Continue Your Education:**
   - Earning additional certifications, degrees, or specialized training can make you more valuable to employers. Whether it's taking courses in leadership, technology, or other areas specific to your industry, continued learning can open the door to higher-paying opportunities.

- Look for scholarships, grants, or employer-sponsored programs to offset the cost of education.
2. **Ask for a Raise or Promotion:**
    - If you've been excelling in your current role, don't be afraid to ask for a raise or promotion. Prepare by gathering evidence of your accomplishments, the value you've added to the company, and any market research that supports your request.
    - Be proactive in expressing your desire for growth and advancement within your company. Employers appreciate employees who are committed to their own development.
3. **Network and Build Relationships:**
    - Networking is critical in many industries. Attend industry events, engage with colleagues and mentors, and look for ways to expand your professional connections. Often, career opportunities come through personal connections rather than job listings.
    - Find a mentor who has already achieved success in your field. They can provide invaluable guidance, advice, and potentially introduce you to lucrative opportunities.
4. **Explore Lateral Moves:**
    - Sometimes, the fastest way to increase your salary is not by climbing up the ladder, but by moving to a new department or company where higher-paying roles are available.

- Lateral moves can offer fresh challenges and new opportunities for growth, allowing you to negotiate for a higher salary.

Step 2: Side Hustles and Freelancing

In today's gig economy, side hustles and freelancing are becoming increasingly popular ways to boost income. Side hustles allow you to earn extra money without quitting your main job, while freelancing can provide more control over your work schedule and the projects you take on.

Popular Side Hustles and Freelance Opportunities:

1. **Freelancing Online:**
   - Platforms like Upwork, Fiverr, and Freelancer offer a variety of freelance opportunities in fields like writing, graphic design, web development, consulting, and more. If you have a skill or talent, you can turn it into a profitable side business by offering services to clients around the world.
   - Build an online portfolio showcasing your work to attract clients, and focus on providing high-quality service to earn repeat business.
2. **E-Commerce:**
   - Starting an online store is a great way to build a business and generate extra income. Whether you're selling handmade goods, dropshipping products,

or flipping items for profit, e-commerce can be a scalable side hustle that fits your lifestyle.
- Platforms like Etsy, eBay, and Shopify make it easier than ever to launch your own online store.

3. **Tutoring or Teaching:**
   - If you're skilled in a subject or have expertise in a particular area, tutoring can be a lucrative side hustle. Whether it's academic tutoring, teaching a language, or providing professional development coaching, many people are willing to pay for your knowledge and guidance.
   - Online tutoring platforms like VIPKid, Chegg, or even offering local lessons can generate significant income.

4. **Ridesharing or Delivery Services:**
   - If you have a car, ridesharing (Uber, Lyft) or food delivery (DoorDash, UberEats) can be a great way to earn extra money on your own schedule.
   - These services provide flexible hours and the ability to work as much or as little as you like, making them ideal for busy individuals.

5. **Real Estate Investment:**
   - Real estate can be a powerful way to boost your income. Whether it's buying rental properties, flipping homes, or investing in real estate investment trusts (REITs), real estate offers opportunities to build wealth through both passive and active income streams.

- Starting small with rental properties can offer consistent cash flow, while flipping homes may provide lump sums of profit when done successfully.

Step 3: Passive Income Streams

While active income (earned from working a job or business) is important, passive income streams are crucial for achieving true financial freedom. Passive income requires less ongoing effort after the initial setup, allowing you to earn money while focusing on other pursuits.

Types of Passive Income Streams:

1. **Dividend Investing:**
    - Investing in dividend-paying stocks can provide you with a regular stream of income without selling your shares. Companies that pay dividends typically do so on a quarterly basis, offering a predictable cash flow.
    - Reinvesting dividends can help you grow your portfolio over time, allowing your wealth to compound.
2. **Rental Income:**
    - Owning rental properties is one of the most popular forms of passive income. By renting out homes, apartments, or even vacation properties, you can earn monthly rental income while the value of your property appreciates.

- If you're just starting out, consider starting with a single property and gradually expanding your portfolio.
3. **Creating Digital Products:**
    - Writing e-books, creating online courses, designing templates, or producing stock photography can generate income long after the initial work is done.
    - Once you create and upload your digital products to a platform like Amazon, Udemy, or Etsy, you can earn money with minimal ongoing effort.
4. **Peer-to-Peer Lending:**
    - Peer-to-peer lending platforms, like LendingClub or Prosper, allow you to lend money to individuals or small businesses in exchange for interest payments.
    - While this involves some risk, it can be a way to earn passive income by acting as a lender rather than a borrower.

Step 4: Investing in Yourself

One of the most impactful ways to maximize your income is by investing in your personal growth and skill development. The more valuable you are to the marketplace, the higher your earning potential.

Ways to Invest in Yourself:

1. **Develop Marketable Skills:**
    - Identify in-demand skills in your industry and invest time in mastering

them. This might involve taking courses in software development, digital marketing, data analysis, or other high-demand fields.
    - Seek out certifications that increase your marketability and open up new career opportunities.
2. **Improve Personal Branding:**
    - Building a strong personal brand can help you stand out in the job market or attract clients to your freelance business. Whether through social media, networking, or creating a personal website, invest in promoting your expertise and building your reputation.
3. **Attend Workshops and Conferences:**
    - Networking events, workshops, and conferences in your field can help you gain knowledge, connect with industry leaders, and discover new opportunities for increasing your income.

Step 5: Diversify Income Sources

Maximizing your income is about more than just boosting one stream—it's about creating multiple streams of income that work together to accelerate your financial freedom.

How to Diversify Your Income:

1. **Create an Investment Strategy:** Diversify your investments across stocks, bonds, real

estate, and other assets to ensure you're earning from multiple sources.
2. **Build Side Businesses:** Instead of relying on a single side hustle, try building multiple businesses or passive income sources that work together.
3. **Leverage Existing Skills:** Look for ways to leverage your current skills in different ways, such as by offering consulting services, creating digital products, or teaching others.

Action Steps for Chapter 9:

1. **Review Your Career:** Look for opportunities to advance your career, ask for a raise, or seek a promotion.
2. **Start a Side Hustle:** Explore freelancing or side businesses that align with your skills and interests.
3. **Create Passive Income Streams:** Research and start building one or more passive income streams that will generate income over time.
4. **Invest in Yourself:** Prioritize learning and skill development to increase your value in the marketplace.
5. **Diversify Your Income:** Work on building multiple income streams to ensure long-term financial security.

Looking Ahead:

Maximizing your income is a powerful tool in achieving financial freedom. In the next chapter, we'll explore how to leverage your income to make smart investments, building long-term wealth that will provide financial freedom for you and your family.

Chapter 10: Smart Investing for Long-Term Wealth

"The goal of investing is not to make quick gains but to create long-term wealth through consistent and disciplined strategies." —Anonymous

Now that you've learned how to maximize your income, it's time to put that extra money to work for you. Smart investing is one of the most effective ways to build long-term wealth and achieve financial freedom. In this chapter, we will explore how to approach investing, the different types of investments, and strategies to ensure that your wealth grows over time.

Understanding the Importance of Investing

Investing is essential for creating wealth because it allows your money to grow over time. Simply saving money in a bank account will not lead to substantial wealth due to inflation eroding the value of cash. Investing, on the other hand, can help you generate returns that outpace inflation and allow you to accumulate wealth passively.

Why Investing is Crucial:

- **Wealth Growth:** Over time, investments have the potential to grow significantly, far beyond what can be achieved through savings alone.
- **Compounding Returns:** By reinvesting your earnings from investments (dividends, interest, capital gains), you allow your wealth to compound, meaning you earn returns on your returns.
- **Beating Inflation:** Investments generally offer returns that outpace inflation, protecting your money's purchasing power.
- **Achieving Financial Freedom:** Investments are the key to generating the passive income streams that lead to financial independence.

Step 1: Start with a Solid Financial Foundation

Before you dive into investing, it's essential to have a solid financial foundation. This ensures that you're prepared to handle any risks and can sustain your investments in the long run.

Key Elements of a Strong Financial Foundation:

1. **Emergency Fund:**
    - Build an emergency fund that covers three to six months' worth of living expenses. This fund acts as a safety net in case of unexpected events like medical bills, job loss, or home repairs.
    - Keep your emergency fund in a liquid, low-risk account, such as a savings account or money market fund.

2. **Pay Off High-Interest Debt:**
   - Before you begin investing, pay off any high-interest debt (e.g., credit card debt). The interest on this type of debt can quickly outpace the returns you may earn from investing, so it's essential to reduce it first.
3. **Know Your Risk Tolerance:**
   - Understand your comfort level with risk. Some people are more comfortable with risky investments that can have high rewards, while others prefer low-risk options with more stable returns. Identifying your risk tolerance will help guide your investment strategy.

Step 2: Diversify Your Investment Portfolio

One of the key principles of investing is diversification—spreading your money across different types of investments. This reduces the risk of a significant loss and provides multiple income streams that can grow over time.

Types of Investments to Consider:

1. **Stocks:**
   - Stocks are shares of ownership in a company. They offer the potential for high returns but come with increased risk, as their value can fluctuate with market conditions.
   - To mitigate risk, diversify your stock holdings by investing in different sectors

(technology, healthcare, finance) and geographic regions (domestic and international markets).

2. **Bonds:**
   - Bonds are loans made to governments or corporations in exchange for periodic interest payments. They are generally less risky than stocks but offer lower returns.
   - Bonds can help stabilize your portfolio by providing regular income and reducing the overall volatility of your investments.

3. **Mutual Funds:**
   - Mutual funds pool money from many investors to invest in a diversified portfolio of stocks, bonds, or other assets. They allow you to invest in a range of assets without having to pick individual investments.
   - Look for low-cost, passively managed funds (such as index funds) that track major market indices.

4. **Exchange-Traded Funds (ETFs):**
   - ETFs are similar to mutual funds but are traded on stock exchanges like individual stocks. They offer low fees and easy diversification, as they hold a variety of assets.
   - ETFs are an excellent choice for beginner investors looking to diversify their portfolios.

5. **Real Estate:**
   - Real estate investments, whether through buying physical property or investing in Real Estate Investment Trusts (REITs),

offer the potential for both income (from rental properties) and appreciation (property value increases).
- Real estate is a great way to diversify outside of traditional stocks and bonds, but it does require more capital and expertise to get started.

6. **Commodities:**
   - Commodities like gold, oil, and agricultural products can be used as a hedge against inflation. They can also offer opportunities for growth when markets are volatile.
   - Investing in commodities can be done through physical ownership, commodity-focused ETFs, or futures contracts.

7. **Cryptocurrency:**
   - Cryptocurrencies like Bitcoin and Ethereum have gained popularity as speculative investments. While they are highly volatile, some investors view them as an opportunity for high returns.
   - Only allocate a small portion of your portfolio to cryptocurrencies due to their high-risk nature.

Step 3: Dollar-Cost Averaging (DCA)

One of the most effective ways to invest is through dollar-cost averaging (DCA). This strategy involves investing a fixed amount of money at regular intervals, regardless of market conditions.

Benefits of Dollar-Cost Averaging:

1. **Mitigating Market Timing Risk:**
   - Timing the market is difficult, and trying to buy low and sell high is not a reliable strategy. DCA helps smooth out market fluctuations and reduces the risk of making poor investment decisions based on short-term market movements.
2. **Consistency:**
   - By investing regularly, you develop a habit of saving and investing, which can contribute significantly to your wealth over time. It encourages a long-term perspective rather than focusing on short-term gains.
3. **Lower Average Cost per Share:**
   - DCA helps to average out the cost of your investments. When the market is down, you buy more shares, and when the market is up, you buy fewer shares. Over time, this can result in a lower average cost per share.

Step 4: Reinvest Earnings and Focus on Compounding

The power of compounding is one of the most powerful wealth-building tools available. Reinvesting your earnings (dividends, interest, capital gains) allows your investments to grow exponentially over time.

How Compounding Works:

- When you reinvest the income you earn from your investments back into your portfolio, you're essentially earning returns on your returns. This accelerates the growth of your wealth and helps your money work harder for you.

Step 5: Avoid Emotional Investing

It's easy to get caught up in market trends and make emotional decisions about your investments. However, emotional investing can lead to buying at the peak of a market and selling when the market is down, which can negatively impact your portfolio.

Tips for Avoiding Emotional Investing:

1. **Stay Disciplined:**
    - Stick to your investment plan and avoid making decisions based on fear or greed. Market fluctuations are normal, and it's important to stay focused on your long-term goals.
2. **Keep a Long-Term Perspective:**
    - Investing is a marathon, not a sprint. Over the long term, the market tends to grow, but there will be periods of volatility. By focusing on your goals and sticking to your strategy, you can weather these ups and downs.
3. **Rebalance Your Portfolio:**
    - Periodically review and rebalance your portfolio to ensure it aligns with your goals and risk tolerance. As some investments grow faster than others,

your portfolio may become unbalanced, so it's important to make adjustments.

Action Steps for Chapter 10:

1. **Build Your Investment Portfolio:** Start investing in stocks, bonds, mutual funds, or real estate, depending on your goals and risk tolerance.
2. **Practice Dollar-Cost Averaging:** Set up regular investment contributions, no matter the market conditions.
3. **Reinvest Your Earnings:** Use the power of compounding to grow your wealth faster by reinvesting dividends, interest, and other earnings.
4. **Stay Disciplined and Avoid Emotional Decisions:** Stick to your long-term investment strategy, and avoid reacting to short-term market volatility.
5. **Diversify Your Investments:** Spread your investments across different asset classes to reduce risk and increase your chances of long-term success.

Conclusion: The Path to Financial Freedom

Achieving financial freedom is not a destination—it's a journey that requires patience, discipline, and a clear understanding of your goals. Throughout this book, we've explored the essential steps needed to gain control over your finances and create a sustainable path toward wealth. Whether you are just starting your financial journey or are looking to optimize your existing strategies, the principles outlined here will help you build a solid foundation for long-term financial success.

Key Takeaways:

1. **Master Your Money:** It all begins with understanding and controlling your income and expenses. By creating a detailed budget, eliminating unnecessary debt, and prioritizing savings, you lay the groundwork for future financial freedom.
2. **Increase Your Income:** Financial freedom is often achieved not just by saving more, but by earning more. Whether through developing new skills, building multiple income streams, or leveraging your assets, increasing your earning power accelerates your journey.
3. **Invest Wisely:** Smart investing allows you to grow your wealth beyond what saving alone can achieve. Diversifying your portfolio, practicing dollar-cost averaging, and reinvesting earnings will help you maximize returns while mitigating risk.
4. **Practice Discipline and Patience:** Building wealth takes time, and it requires consistency. By sticking to a well-thought-out plan, avoiding

emotional investing, and staying focused on your long-term goals, you will see the fruits of your efforts.
5. **Guard Your Wealth:** Financial freedom is not just about accumulating money; it's also about protecting it. Insurance, estate planning, and risk management ensure that you safeguard your wealth for the future, protecting you from unexpected events that could derail your progress.

The Bigger Picture:

Financial freedom means more than just the ability to live without financial stress—it's about the freedom to live life on your own terms. It's about having the flexibility to choose how you spend your time, to invest in the things that matter most to you, and to have the peace of mind that comes with financial security.

By taking control of your finances, making informed decisions, and committing to the principles of smart money management, you'll be able to create a future that aligns with your values and aspirations.

Remember, the road to financial freedom may not always be easy, but with determination, knowledge, and a clear plan, you can overcome obstacles and achieve the life you've always dreamed of.

Your Financial Freedom Journey Begins Today

The journey towards financial freedom starts with the first step—taking control of your finances and committing to the process. The habits you build, the knowledge you gain, and the steps you take will shape your financial future. Don't wait for the perfect moment; start now, and take consistent action toward a future of financial independence and security.

As you continue on this journey, always remember that financial freedom is not just about money—it's about the freedom to live the life you desire, without the constraints of financial stress. Embrace the process, stay committed to your goals, and you will find that financial freedom is within reach.

Bibliography

1. **Bogle, John C.** *The Little Book of Common Sense Investing: The Only Way to Guarantee Your Fair Share of Stock Market Returns.* John Wiley & Sons, 2007.
2. **Kiyosaki, Robert T.** *Rich Dad Poor Dad: What the Rich Teach Their Kids About Money That the Poor and Middle Class Do Not.* Warner Books, 2000.
3. **Orman, Suze.** *The Money Book for the Young, Fabulous & Broke.* Spiegel & Grau, 2005.
4. **Ramsey, Dave.** *The Total Money Makeover: A Proven Plan for Financial Fitness.* Thomas Nelson, 2009.
5. **Sethi, Ramit.** *I Will Teach You to Be Rich.* Workman Publishing Company, 2009.
6. **Clark, Roberta, and Jerry V. White.** *Money Sense for Kids: A Guide to Financial Literacy for Young People.* Kogan Page, 2004.
7. **Collins, Craig.** *The Simple Path to Wealth: Your Road Map to Financial Independence and a Rich, Free Life.* CreateSpace, 2016.
8. **Fitzgerald, Joe.** *Financial Freedom: A Proven Path to All the Money You Will Ever Need.* McGraw-Hill Education, 2020.
9. **Schwab, Charles.** *The Charles Schwab Guide to Financial Independence: How to Build Wealth, Achieve Financial Freedom, and Live Your Best Life.* Wiley, 2019.
10. **Towers, David.** *The Psychology of Money: Timeless Lessons on Wealth, Greed, and Happiness.* Harriman House, 2020.

www.ingramcontent.com/pod-product-compliance
Lightning Source LLC
Chambersburg PA
CBHW071108240526
45469CB00006BD/2381